GO FACTS ENVIRONMENTAL ISSUES
Conservation

Conservation

contents

© 2006 Blake Publishing
Additional material © A & C Black Publishers Ltd 2007

First published in Australia by Blake Education Pty Ltd.

This edition published in the United Kingdom in 2007 by
A & C Black Publishers Ltd, 38 Soho Square, London, W1D 3HB.
www.acblack.com

Hardback edition
ISBN 978-0-7136-7962-5

Paperback edition
ISBN 978-0-7136-7970-0

A CIP record for this book is available from the British Library.

Author: Ian Rohr
Publisher: Katy Pike
Editor: Mark Stafford
Design and layout by The Modern Art Production Group

Image credits: p8 (t)—The Wilderness Society; p10 (b), p11 (all)—Paul McEvoy; p15 (b), p17 (bl)—AAP; p21 (br)—Clean Up Australia; p25 (tl)—NASA.

Printed in China by WKT Company Ltd.

This book is produced using paper that is made from wood grown in managed sustainable forests. It is natural, renewable and recyclable. The logging and manufacturing processes conform to the environmental regulations of the country of origin.

Planet under Threat

The Earth's natural resources sustain the many diverse forms of life on the planet. But humans are polluting and exhausting those resources.

Natural resources

Our natural resources are forests, water, soil, minerals, plants, animals and **fossil fuels**. Some natural resources can be partly renewed; for example, forests can be replanted and soil damage can be repaired. Other resources are not **renewable**; when they are all used up, they will be gone forever.

Damaging the environment

Carbon dioxide is a gas that occurs naturally in the atmosphere. The amount of carbon dioxide in the atmosphere is increasing because people are removing forests, which absorb carbon dioxide, and burning fossil fuels, which generates carbon dioxide. Increased carbon dioxide has caused the Earth's atmosphere and oceans to heat up. This is called **global warming**.

Many animal and plant species have become endangered as their natural habitats continue to be destroyed. Fresh water in rivers and lakes is under threat from irrigation, which reduces the flow of water, and soil run-off which contains chemical fertilisers and pesticides.

Conservation and sustainability

What can be done to help the planet? Conservation is choosing to not use up or **contaminate** the planet's natural resources. It is working to protect, restore and sustain our environment.

Sustainability is using the planet's resources in a responsible and planned way so that they will last longer. It is development that benefits the current generation without disadvantaging future generations.

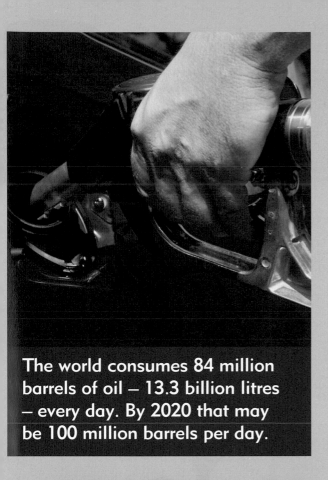

The world consumes 84 million barrels of oil – 13.3 billion litres – every day. By 2020 that may be 100 million barrels per day.

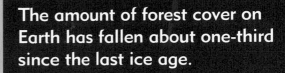

The amount of forest cover on Earth has fallen about one-third since the last ice age.

Nearly 16 000 species of animals and plants are threatened with extinction.

GO FACT!
DID YOU KNOW?

Natural resources are not used equally around the world. A person in a Western nation, such as the UK, Australia or the USA, consumes as much of the world's resources as 30–40 people in a developing nation, such as Kenya, Guatemala or Cambodia.

5

Forests

A forest is an **ecosystem** dominated by trees. Forests cover about 30 per cent of the Earth's land surface.

Types of forest

There are three main types of forest: tropical forests (including rainforests), temperate forests and boreal forests.

Tropical forests grow in areas of high rainfall. They consist of tall trees, which form a **canopy**, and layers of shorter trees between the tallest trees and the ground. The Amazon rainforest in South America contains one-third of the world's trees.

Temperate forests contain mostly broad-leafed, **deciduous** trees with some **conifers**. They occur in warm, rainy climates.

Boreal forests consist of needle-leafed, **evergreen** conifers, such as pine trees. They grow in areas with short summers and long winters. Whereas rainforests contain many animal species, boreal forests have mainly birds and mammals, such as deer, wolves and rodents, and very few reptiles.

Forests and the planet

Forests play an important role in helping to stabilise the Earth's climate. Forest trees absorb carbon dioxide and produce oxygen through a process known as **photosynthesis**.

Forests also help to stabilise the soil and prevent **erosion** by controlling the run-off of water after it rains. Without forests, a lot of soil, valuable for farming, can wash into waterways.

Tropical   **Temperate**   **Boreal**

Tropical rainforests cover only six per cent of the Earth's land surface but contain more than half the planet's plant and animal species.

The world may be losing as much as 170 000 square kilometres of tropical forest every year – that is equivalent to 40 football fields per minute. People cut down trees to make paper and other wood products, or burn the forest to clear it for farming land.

7

Sustainable Forests?

Forests play an important role in the health of the planet, but we continue to cut them down. Is it possible to use forests without destroying them?

What do forests mean to people?

Forests mean different things to different people. To the native people of Brazil, the forest is their home. A logging company sees a forest as a source of timber. For a logging worker, it is a place to work and earn a living. To someone living in a city, a forest might be a place to find peace and relaxation. For governments of developing nations, forests provide products to export, and people with land for farming.

For and against

Logging companies argue that forests are a renewable resource to use in a sustainable way – new trees can be planted to replace the ones removed. The logging industry employs many people, and logging produces things that people want, such as timber, paper, tissue, cardboard and furniture.

Conservationists say that forests, especially tropical rainforests, are vital to the health of the planet. They want logging in 'old growth forests' – the mature forests that have not been disturbed by people – to stop because forest ecosystems are damaged by logging. They argue that trees should only be logged from plantation forests, which are 'tree farms' grown especially to be cut down for wood products. Conservationists believe that people working in the old-growth logging industry could find jobs in the plantation timber and tourism industries.

Tasmanian forests have the tallest flowering plants on Earth, with trees reaching over 90 metres in the Styx Valley.

Image: The Wilderness Society

Logging is so widespread in Brazil that the only way of measuring it is by using satellites in space.

Timber is one of the few natural building materials – it is non-toxic, safe to handle and doesn't break down into environmentally damaging materials.

Plant Your Own Forest

Plant your own miniature tropical rainforest.

You will need:

- large glass container or plastic jar with lid
- potting mix
- some indoor plants
- charcoal
- fine gravel
- pebbles
- strong, thick rubber band
- clear plastic wrap or plastic sheet.

2 Add a layer of potting mix and plant the plants.

1 Place in the jar: 1st – 2.5 centimetre layer of pebbles, 2nd – 2.5 centimetre layer of charcoal, 3rd – 2.5 centimetre layer of gravel.

3 Put on the lid or stretch the plastic over the top. Use the rubber band to hold the plastic in place.

After a few days, the plastic or lid will be covered with water droplets, which will fall back to the soil and seep down to the plants' roots.

Protection in Parks

National parks, reserves and other protected areas are created to conserve the plants, animals and natural features within their boundaries.

Pathway to parks

Protected areas vary from small reserves that protect a specific habitat or species, to vast parks covering thousands of square miles and containing many ecosystems.

The idea of protected natural areas became popular in the early 1800s. In 1864, US President Abraham Lincoln signed a law that gave Yosemite Valley to the state of California to be 'held for public use, resort and recreation'. In 1872, the world's first national park was created: Yellowstone National Park, in the USA. This was followed by the Royal National Park in Sydney, Australia, in 1879, and national parks in Canada and New Zealand.

Growing numbers

After World War II, the number of national parks grew rapidly. The United Nations began establishing World Heritage Areas in 1975, to protect some of the world's natural and built wonders – by 2005 there were 812 sites.

There are now more than 102 000 national parks, wilderness reserves, heritage sites and other protected areas around the world. They cover almost 20 million square kilometres of land – an area larger than Canada, the United States and Germany combined.

Popular Parks	Approximate number of visitors per year
Fuji-Hakone-Izu National Park, Japan	100 million
Peak District National Park, Great Britain	22 million
Great Smoky Mountain National Park, USA	9.3 million
Banff National Park, Canada	5 million
Kosciusko National Park, Australia	3 million

Australia's Great Barrier Reef is the largest United Nations World Heritage Site.

North East Greenland National Park is the largest in the world at 972 000 square kilometres, which is about the same size as Egypt.

GO FACT!

DID YOU KNOW?

Approximately one-third of mainland New Zealand is protected in parks and reserves.

13

When Land Becomes Sick

Healthy, productive land can become dry and salty because of the way people use two natural resources: soil and water.

Losing soil

Trees and other plants bind soil together with their root systems. When too much native vegetation is removed – such as when land is cleared to graze animals – the structure of the soil breaks down. It dries out and erodes, either blown away by the wind or carried away by rain.

Soil can become **compacted** by overgrazing from cattle and other **domesticated** animals. Compacted soil does not absorb water easily, so crops miss out on the water and nutrients the rain brings.

Salinity

Dryland **salinity** occurs when deep-rooted plants, such as trees and native grasses, are cleared from the land and replaced with shallow-rooted crops and pastures. The shallow-rooted crops do not absorb as much rain as the deep-rooted plants, so the water seeps down to the **saline watertable** below the plants. This causes the level of the watertable to rise, and the salt that it contains kills most plants.

Without vegetation, the bare, salty soil erodes and is washed into rivers. For people who rely on rivers for their fresh water, the water becomes undrinkable.

Although soil erosion and damage is not as dramatic as earthquakes or hurricanes, their effect on the land can be just as devastating.

GO FACT!
DID YOU KNOW?
Up to 15 million hectares of farming land in Australia could be lost to salinity within the next 50 years.

Erosion gullies form when fast-moving water is not absorbed by vegetation and instead carves out soil – the more it rains, the wider and deeper the gully becomes.

Desertification – turning farming land into desert – is caused by over-clearing, overgrazing and over-cultivating land, usually on the edge of natural deserts. It can lead to massive dust storms, where the top layer of soil is blown away.

Healing the Land

Soil damage can be repaired by finding what caused the damage and reversing the process.

Fighting salinity

Replanting the trees and other deep-rooted plants that were cleared for farming reduces salinity. Trees are planted as small seedlings. Australian native species can grow from seedlings to four metres high in only 18 months, depending on the quality of the soil. Trees have a better chance of surviving if they are species adapted to the local soil and climate.

Another way to reduce salinity is to switch to deep-rooted crops, such as alfalfa, and salt-tolerant crops and grasses.

Perennial crops can help reduce soil salinity because they leak less water beneath the **root zone** than **annual** crops. New industries might take advantage of the salty soil by using the saline ground water for fish farms, or even harvesting salt to eat.

Conservation farming

Rather than trying to reverse soil damage, conservation farming reduces the likelihood that it will be damaged in the first place. Conservation farming is also known as 'no till' farming because it involves not ploughing the soil too often, and leaving the remains of harvested crops on the ground to protect the soil.

This allows the soil to retain water, which greatly reduces erosion. Conservation farming also saves the fuel needed by machines to remove crop remains.

Terracing has been used for thousands of years to reduce soil erosion on sloping ground.

Saltbush is a salt-tolerant plant that can be eaten by sheep, making it a useful crop to grow while other plants are establishing themselves.

Groves of trees are planted between fields as windbreaks to prevent wind erosion.

17

Industries make products and materials, such as electricity and petrol, which provide us with a modern, comfortable way of life – but they also pollute our natural resources.

Air pollution

The major sources of industrial air pollution are chemical plants, power stations, oil refineries and factories. However, cars pollute the air as much as industries do.

Under certain weather conditions, several air **pollutants** can have a combined effect that is worse than their individual effects. An example is photochemical

smog, sometimes seen as a white haze over cities during summer. Photochemical smog forms on still days when sunlight causes chemical reactions between chemicals in the air. A product of

these reactions is ozone, a gas harmful to people, animals and plants.

Soil and water pollution

Soil can be contaminated by **pesticides**, **herbicides** and **heavy metals**. Contaminated soil is carried into local waterways, as run-off from rain, and eventually ends up in oceans. Liquid industrial waste is sometimes dumped directly into waterways. This leads to a build-up of poisons in local food chains.

For example, dioxins are poisonous waste products from making pesticides, paper, plastic and steel. Dioxins can leak into the environment and build up in animals and people that come into contact with them.

Ozone attacks the tissues of the throat and lungs and irritates the eyes.

Toxic tars, oils and ash were buried at old gas manufactur[ing] plants. Former plants must be decontaminated before the land can be used safely.

High levels of dioxins found in fish populations can shut down local fishing industries.

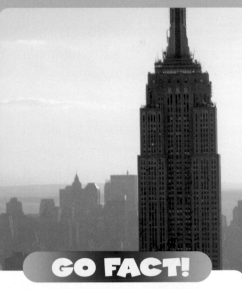

GO FACT!

DID YOU KNOW?

Visibility in the eastern United States should improve by 30 per cent as **emissions** from power stations are dramatically cut.

Controlling Pollution

We all suffer from the effects of pollution – but who is responsible for stopping it or cleaning it up?

Policing pollution

Most countries have anti-pollution controls. There are laws to limit the amount of pollutants released into the atmosphere, and dumping industrial waste can lead to heavy fines. These laws are enforced by government bodies, such as the Environmental Protection Agency.

Anti-pollution laws are not always enough to deter a company from polluting because the fines for breaking the laws are often small compared to a company's wealth.

Cleaner power plants

Almost all of our electricity comes from burning fossil fuels: coal, natural gas and oil. Power companies can make burning coal a cleaner process by washing the coal before burning it. They can also burn a type of coal that contains less pollution-producing sulphur, or use devices called 'scrubbers' to remove sulphur dioxide from the gas that leaves the power plant.

Change in the air

Individuals can also have a major effect on reducing pollution. While power companies can burn coal more cleanly, people can use less electricity and choose 'green power' – electricity that comes from non-polluting sources, such as hydro-electricity and wind farms.

It requires the combined efforts of individuals, companies and governments to reduce pollution.

A car engine that is properly tuned will emit up to 25 per cent less pollution than a poorly maintained one.

The Brown Cloud – air pollution three kilometres thick that stretches through Asia and the Middle East – is the result of industries, cars, forest fires and household stoves.

After the Exxon Valdez oil tanker spilt 50 million litres of oil along the Alaskan coast, Exxon Mobil Corporation spent $6 billion on fines and $4 billion to clean up the spill and settle court claims.

Australia's Community Clean Up campaign started in 1989 to remove litter from Sydney Harbour. Clean Up Australia Day is now held every year, and run in 120 other countries as "Clean Up the World".

No More Plastic Bags!

Supermarket plastic bags are convenient, but they are made from natural resources and they damage the environment when they are thrown away.

Death in the ocean

Plastic bags are made from high-density polyethylene, a type of plastic. It takes 1.75 kilograms of oil – a non-renewable natural resource – to make one kilogram of plastic bags.

Discarded plastic bags become general litter and block drains. Bags that end up in the ocean are mistaken for jellyfish by turtles and other marine creatures. Once eaten, the bag blocks the animal's digestive tract, so it slowly starves to death.

In the UK, 10 billion plastic bags are used each year – 167 bags for each person in the country.

Most bags end up in landfills, where they will take up to 1000 years to break down, or in waterways and oceans.

Bin the bags

The solution to plastic bag pollution is fairly simple. Stop using them!

Conservationists want retailers to offer alternatives, such as reusable shopping bags. They also want shoppers to refuse plastic bags and use the alternatives. Many major supermarkets in the UK have already begun to introduce reusable bag schemes.

If you must use plastic shopping bags, reuse them rather than throwing them away.

Only 7 per cent of the UK's plastic bags are recycled, even though there are recycling bins at major supermarkets.

Discarded plastic bags kill 100 000 birds, whales, seals and turtles every year.

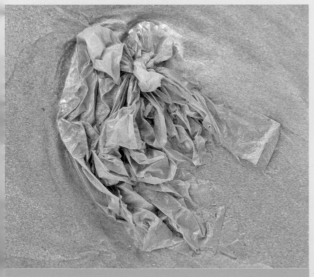

Plastic bags were banned in Dhaka, capital of Bangladesh, after millions of littered plastic bags blocked the city's drainage system and stopped flood waters draining away.

Australia's first 'Plastic Bag Free Town' was Coles Bay in Tasmania. Since April 2003, all shops have banned plastic bags.

Coles Bay
Tasmania
Australia's First
Plastic Bag Free Town
PLANETARK

Living in a Greenhouse

The Earth is wrapped in an **insulating** blanket of gases that acts like a greenhouse in a garden. High levels of some gases are making the greenhouse overheat.

A **natural greenhouse**

The Earth's insulating **greenhouse gases** include carbon dioxide and methane. They trap heat from the sun, making the planet about 30 °C warmer than it would otherwise be. Without the natural greenhouse effect it would be too cold for life as we know it to exist on Earth.

A **runaway greenhouse**

Human activities have increased the amount of greenhouse gases. Burning fossil fuels releases carbon dioxide into the atmosphere, and clearing vegetation also increases levels of greenhouse gases because plants absorb carbon dioxide – fewer plants means more carbon dioxide.

Carbon dioxide levels have risen dramatically in the last 30 years, warming the Earth's atmosphere and oceans and changing weather patterns. Most scientists agree that global warming is already taking place. Between 1996 and 2005, the world experienced nine of the ten warmest years on record.

To stop global warming will require reductions in greenhouse pollution. People will need to drastically change the way they use and produce energy. Burning fossil fuels is the largest source of greenhouse gases, and alternative energy sources need to be developed.

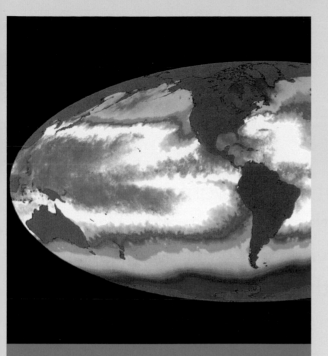

Scientists measure sea temperatures to help detect changes in the Earth's temperature.

30 per cent of carbon dioxide released into the atmosphere is from the burning of tropical rainforests.

Australia produces more greenhouse gas emissions per person than any other country because about 80 per cent of its electricity comes from burning coal.

Global warming could extend the range of mosquitoes, and assist the spread of malaria, Ross River fever, Dengue fever and Yellow fever to areas previously too cold for mosquitoes.

25

Climate Change and You

Scientists predict that global warming will cause massive changes to the environment. These changes will affect everyone – where they live, how they travel and the cost of living.

Massive change

It is difficult to predict the exact effects of global warming. How quickly the climate changes will depend on the level of greenhouse gas emissions, and how sensitive the climate is to those emissions.

Extremes of weather have been predicted – more frequent and intense heatwaves, storms, floods and droughts. Farms could yield fewer crops. Rising ocean levels, from melting ice caps, could force millions of people from their homes.

One study has predicted that if nothing is done to reduce greenhouse gas emissions, the global average temperature will increase by 3 °C by 2080. If Greenland's climate was to warm this much, the massive icesheet that has covered the area for thousands of years would melt and raise world sea levels by around seven metres.

Animals and plants

Though some plant and animal species would prosper as a result of temperature changes, many would become extinct as their habitats altered under the changed conditions.

An increase in ocean temperatures of as little as 1 °C or 2 °C above the normal summer maximum can cause coral reefs to suffer from heat stress and 'bleach'. Australia's Great Barrier Reef – and the marine life and tourism industry it supports – could be severely damaged within 30 years.

Global warming may cause tropical cyclones to become more powerful, although maybe not more numerous.

Rainfall records from England and Wales dating back to 1766 show that there is now more rain in winter (especially heavy rain) but less rain in summer.

A European **heatwave** in 2003 killed 20 000 people and caused great losses in agricultural productivity. Human activities are increasing the likelihood of such extreme weather events.

GO FACT!

DID YOU KNOW?
Between 2002 and 2005 Antarctica's ice melted faster than it was replaced by new snow.

Renewable Energy

We rely overwhelmingly on coal, oil and natural gas to give us power. These resources are finite – there are limited reserves of them on Earth. Our future requires renewable sources of energy.

The need for power

Fossil fuels supply most of the world's energy, and will probably do so for many years – but not forever. Oil production is declining in 33 of the 48 largest oil producing countries, yet demand for energy is increasing as nations develop and economies grow. Easily available energy promotes **economic development**, which then creates demand for still more energy.

Energy Earth

Our planet is a powerhouse of energy, waiting to be harnessed. Waves, water, wind and sunshine are all forms of renewable energy that can be used to generate electricity. The use of solar power is expanding as technology improves and it becomes cheaper to produce. Commercial wind turbines harness energy in more than 65 countries, making wind power the world's fastest-growing source of energy after solar. Geothermal energy – literally 'heat from the earth' – has become an important energy source in several countries.

A new energy market

To develop these technologies so that they contribute more of the world's energy requires people to ask for clean, renewable energy. This will encourage companies and governments to invest in renewable energy industries and therefore reduce our dependence on fossil fuels.

Using only six per cent of the USA's area to produce wind power would generate 1.5 times the nation's present power consumption.

Solar panels have no moving parts, require minimal maintenance, take up little space and make no noise.

Geothermal power provides heating and electricity for nearly 90 per cent of Iceland's population.

Biomass energy fuels include agricultural leftovers, such as bagasse (sugar cane residue), rice hulls, peanut shells, vineyard clippings, wheat straw, corn leaves, stalks and cobs.

Ten Ways to 'Go Green'

It's easy to 'go green'. If we all try to conserve natural resources, we will make a real difference to the planet's future.

1. Ask your parents to install a water-efficient shower head.

2. Start a compost heap.

3. Use both sides of a sheet of paper before recycling it.

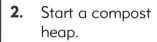

4. Keep a bottle of water in the fridge, instead of running the tap until the water is cool.

5. Turn lights, computers and other appliances off if they're not being used.

6. When brushing your teeth, use a glass of water instead of leaving the tap running.

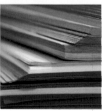

7. Ride a bike or walk instead of asking Mum or Dad for a lift.

8. Join a local environmental group.

9. Put a 'No junk mail, thanks' sticker on your letterbox.

10. Avoid items that are designed to be used only once — foam cups, paper plates, plastic cutlery.

Glossary

annual plant that lives for only one growing season

canopy the branches and leaves that spread out at the top of a group of trees

carbon dioxide (chemical symbol: CO_2) a colourless, odourless gas found in the atmosphere. In its solid form it is known as 'dry ice'.

compacted closely and firmly packed together

conifer tree or shrub that produces seeds in cones

conservationist someone who works to protect the environment

contaminate to make impure or unsafe by adding pollutants

deciduous plants that shed their leaves at the end of the growing season (usually in autumn)

domesticated animals or plants that are controlled by people to provide food, power or companionship

economic development the growth of a country or region's economy

ecosystem a community of species interacting with each other and the environment

emissions the release of gases from industries and transport

erosion the wearing away of the Earth's surface by water, wind and ice

evergreen trees that keep their leaves throughout the entire year

fossil fuels fuels formed from the remains of plants and organisms that died millions of years ago; especially oil, coal and natural gas

global warming an increase in the average temperature of the Earth's atmosphere and oceans

greenhouse gases carbon dioxide, ozone, methane, nitrous oxide and water vapour. These gases trap heat from the sun and warm the atmosphere.

heatwave a long period of very hot weather

heavy metals metals that are often present in small amounts in humans and animals, but cause illness if present in large amounts

herbicide a chemical used to kill plants (especially weeds) or inhibit their growth

insulating stopping heat, sound or electricity from escaping or entering

perennial a plant lasting for three growing seasons or more

pesticide a chemical used to kill pests, such as insects and rodents

photosynthesis the process by which a plant uses the energy from the light of the sun to produce its own food

pollutants waste materials that damage the water, air or soil

renewable capable of being renewed or replaced, so it won't run out

root zone the area immediately surrounding the roots and from which a plant gets water and nourishment

saline containing salt

salinity the saltiness of a substance

watertable the underground level below which the ground is saturated with water

Index